Chasing the Roots of my Heritage

Randall Simone Gregory

First paperback edition: May 2021

Book cover design by: Saqib Mushtaq

Illustrated pages by: Venessa Kaiser

Imprint: Her Legacy, LLC

ISBN: 9798592929915

DEDICATION POEM

To:

The Illustrious Clark Atlanta University
all the HBCU Grads/Alumni/Alumnae
the parents that took out loans to send us here
HBCU lovers
HBCU admirers
current students
black excellence
future students
every reader
everyone that supports me
my forever family I've made at CAU
my beloved professors
all the HBCUs still standing and the ones that have fallen
my classmates, we did it
my friends, I can't wait to see all your dreams come true
my sisters, aunties, uncles, cousins, niece and grandparents, I love you all
my phenomenal parents, thank you for everything. I hope it was money
well spent

"Here's to my journey at THE BEST HBCU"...

TABLE OF CONTENTS

Chasing the Roots of my Heritage

FORWARD

by Basheer Jones
Poet, Motivational Speaker, Morehouse Man, Social
Activist and Cleveland Councilman

Growing up in Cleveland, Ohio is no easy feat. I know that everyone says that about their city, but if you're from Cleveland you know exactly what I'm talking about. Despite our struggles, we are home to the first black mayor, Carl Stokes, of a major metropolitan city. Home of Superman, Rock and Roll Hall of Fame, and this amazing Clark Atlanta University and Beaumont grad, Randall Gregory. As a graduate of Morehouse College, I can tell you first hand that the HBCU experience is unlike no other. Seeing black excellence on a daily basis, not only brings out the best of you, but it is truly inspiring.

HBCUs have their challenges, but their blessings surely outweighs them. In this book, our Poet Laureate, Randall Gregory will take you on a journey through her experience in the Atlanta University Center as a student at CAU. I graduated from Morehouse College in 2006 and was the founder of a very popular poetry night called "AUC Jazzmans Poetry Night" which lasted for years after I graduated. What I miss most about the event, was how ideas flowed from the lips of black people from all across the country. We must tell our own story or it will be told for us. I'm thankful that Randall has decided to tell her story, which is a part of the collective story of the black experience in America. Thank you for your courage Randall! I hope her words will inspire you to tell your story one day soon! God bless you all.

-Basheer Jones

"Knowing all that we are unlocks our power within"

-R.S.G

This is for The Culture...

Négritude

There's magic in our melanin
that's why they tried to dispel us

there's power in our voices
that's why they tried to silence us

there's enlightenment in our education
that's why they tried to deny us

there's insight in our reading
that's why they tried to ban us

there's survival in our bodies
that's why they pretended to cure us

there's strength in our heritage
that's why they tried to erase us

there's royalty in our roots
that's why they tried to diminish us

there's resilience in our D-N-A
and that's why they can't break us

* Négritude: the affirmation or consciousness of the value of black or African culture, heritage, and identity.

Randall Simone Gregory

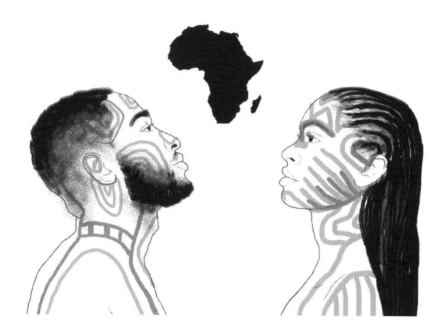

I'll Find a Way or Make One

A declaration
a cultural creed
an unparalleled motto
what I live by to-this-day
it is THEE standard
the essence of a black panther
the artistry of finesse
the epitome of perseverance
it's defying odds
going against gravity
when the world pulls you down
it's self-determination
triumph and victory

not sulking in the noes
but calculating your next steps
putting in the work
while trusting God is ahead
the endurance that kicks in
even when you're tired

for every door closed
it's locating the key
or
finding another entrance
buying the building, if necessary

just know
regardless of life's circumstances

I'll find a way
or
make one
and no one can stop me

I, Too, Am American

I am the darker sister.

They tell me to go back to Africa

When they feel threatened by my existence

But I laugh at their ignorance,

And shake my head,

Becoming more resilient.

Tomorrow,

I'll walk in the building,

And no one will dare

Say to me,

"Go back to Africa"

Then.

Besides,

They'll recognize this land I was born on

The land my ancestors were forced to cultivate and stay on

They'll see how beautiful I am

They'll be ashamed and realize-

I, too, am American.

*With thanks to fellow HBCU grad, Langston Hughes.
This is a copy change poem based on "I, Too, sing America."

The Decision

I keep checking the mail
looking out the window
as if I'm waiting on a precious package
hoping
it makes its way
no sign
no word
of what's to come
all I can do is pray

it's here-
what holds my fate inside
tearing open the envelope

inhaling a big breath
with my eyes closed
I pull out the letter
that will change the trajectory of my life
as I exhale slowly
I open my eyes wide
as I scan the paper carefully
there's one thing I see

Congratulations!
my dream school chose ME
I got my acceptance letter

I
am
blessed
and
I am happy
and
I am ready

Admitted Day

A day
colleges show off their best features

a day
campus chefs put their feet all in the food
serving us the best of the best
fulfilling home cooked meals

heartfelt messages
inspiring testimonies shared
encouraging words
to lead us back here

giveaways
raffles
free t-shirts
and fun

in awe of everything I see
group tours
black excellence
a historic campus
and all the future students in sight

feeling like family
on day one
it's confirmed
I know
I belong here
this IS the community
I must be a part of

Premeditated

I'm learning to deprive my insecurities
hoping that one day they up and leave
they hit *67 before they call every morning
I stopped picking up knowing it's them
"do not disturb" until they grow tired of trying to reach me
when I catch them sleeping, I silence them with a pillow
I smother them with uplift
when I find them dancing, I turn off the music
I hold them prisoner in the basement of my thoughts
wishing loneliness will lead to their escape
when they leave clues behind, I follow them like a relentless detective
trying to discover where their origins began
when they resurface around friends, we play Russian Roulette
patiently waiting for them to catch a bullet
when I go out, I poison them with liquor
they take shots, and I drown them in self-doubt
praying they become unsure of my address
they return to my home
and I invite them back in
so when they have newfound comfortability
I tie them up and tell them about the trip we'll be taking
I put them in the car while it's running
leaving the garage door down
as we get high off carbon monoxide
I dial 911

hello operator,
something has happened and no, it wasn't an accident

Grilled Cheese

At an HBCU
the cafeteria is lovingly called "the cafe"
a place of comfort and solace

the cafeteria staff feel like
mamas
aunties
uncles
cousins
and close friends

every time I saw the grill master
he greeted me like he'd known me all my life
never seeming to miss work
flipping burgers with precision
food cooked to perfection
always with a big smile on his face

after my first few weeks
he lovingly nicknamed me "Grilled Cheese"

oh how I loved those warm buttery slices of bread
with thick layers of melted cheese inside
it's like he could read my mind cause it was always made just
right

my senior year
the cafe grill master finally asked my real name
it only lasted a day…
I walk up to the counter the next day
he had already forgotten my name
"Hey Grilled Cheese"
shouting loud and proud
I smile back
we exchange pleasantries
ever since I was a freshman
he always remembered
my ultimate favorite thing to order
maybe he didn't forget my name at all
I think he realized just how much I adored being called
"Grilled Cheese"

Orientation

My time has arrived
I made it here
I'm ready for the new life
I'm about to live
five days seem so long
missing my family already
even though they just dropped me off

early mornings
schedules full of what we'd do
the OGs
appearing to be the coolest people on campus
talking to some new people
attending some boring stuff
connecting with people from my major
running around
collecting signatures mandatory for freshman seminar
or so they said
adjusting to dorm life

I learned the campus quickly
we danced
learned chants
repped our cities
discovered
which sides were the crunkest
gained mentors
attended St. Jude

taught us our history and heritage
informed us of what would come next

the ups
the downs
and everything in-between
started friendships for life
they watered our roots
I felt myself sprout
a lot of growth
from here and now
I'm prepared
for the journey ahead
I'm ready for college to begin

Induction

All white dresses
flesh tone tights
crisp white button-downs
fresh pressed suits
and solid ties

this is a day
to celebrate an accomplishment
five long days have passed
though it felt like two weeks
we ruled the campus
on our own
we have learned what it takes
to be a member of this "oh so fine" institution

in a procession
we march up the hill
dress shoes and heels
making music
with every step
click clacking
against the pavement

a long walk to the gym
we walk with pride
the torch of new beginnings lit
we stand in unison
taking an oath
of solidarity
promising to become
who we want to be
regardless of the challenges that come our way

now crowned
new members of the kingdom
time to be leaders
and become risk-takers
ready to face the world
now, let the history begin

Freshman Seminar

A required course
mandatory history to be embraced
captivated by countless stories that baptized our ears with richness
us not knowing is no longer an excuse
filled with black excellence
flowing with our black history

running around
completing lyceums
getting flyers signed
attending countless events

elders testing our understanding
filling our minds with golden facts
miraculous untold truths
solidifying the bedrock of our cultural knowledge
planted heritage and roots for miles

if outsiders question us
we can educate them with the quickness
learning on top of learning
the fight song-rehearsed it!
our motto-learned it!
the colors-till this day!
the importance of the seal- etched understanding!
and the impact of others-our brave history makers!
Just ask...we can name them all

instilled cultural pride
awakened community activism
that lasts a lifetime
through learning
without us realizing
a class most of us didn't want to take

opened our minds
poured in authentic love
nurtured our greatness

bred in all of us

First Day

Look in the mirror 1,000 times
to confirm I look good

got on the FIT I picked out last night
you can't tell me anything
I mean, nothin'

trying to decide what time I should leave
don't want to be too early
but... early enough to find a seat

feeling proud and prominent
like a personal stylist dressed me
picking your first-day FIT is major
purely paramount
a cultural tradition
in our community
what is understood you don't explain

people won't know your name
so your clothes do all the talking

my class is in the busiest building on campus
it's way more people than I expected

it's my first day
here goes nothing...I mean here goes everything

Where an HBCU Can Take you

Imagine what your life could be
when your wildest dreams come true
that is where an HBCU can take you
perfectly prepped for the office
poised for the grand stage
prepared for the operating room
producing day time and prime time

an HBCU can take you
to the courtroom
the grand prix
CEO corner office

an HBCU can take you
around the world
don't let anyone discourage you
you will soar every height you wish to reach

it can even take you to the White House

So when someone asks...

Where can an HBCU *degree take* you?
don't tell them about the immeasurable cultural competence
nor about the HBCU fortress that is built to prepare you
the proud legacy that was poured inside you
how not to assimilate but how to accelerate
the stellar education that was bestowed upon you

Just say…

On TOP of the WORLD
EVERYWHERE you can go
even to places that aren't built yet

Olive Branch

There were three trees
when they were just seeds
they were planted close together
but far enough away for them to grow freely
without restriction
each tree
branches were filled with olives
to nurture all those that visited
and those who came in contact
their roots
anchored
wound in the rich soil
there was unwavering peace
when people walked amongst the trees
there was unity
amongst the fibrous differences
thousands of years passed
as they grew in various directions
the olive branches touched
etched in the trunk
connection
reconciliation
respect
love

there is so much power in those trees
the olives
the branches
that grew in a community

I Hit the Lotto

I hit the jackpot
the biggest one yet
there's so much I want
and
so much I need
I'll make a budget
of how the money will be spent
no longer broke
I might splurge
a little
spoil myself
a bit
I deserve the world
I can't wait
to cash
my refund check

Psalm 30

When the world feels like it's ending

I go to sleep

and when I wake up

I have another opportunity

I'm so grateful

that I'm alive

so

joy

came this morning

Finding Courage

The caged bird

who dreams

yet

afraid to sing

hoping one day

it finds the audacity to use its wings

and break free

The Journey Ahead

*This is a two-voice poem, please read from left to right across both pages

College bound student 1

I am getting ready for college

most people on campus don't look
like me

I am here to receive a great education

I am placed in remedial classes to make sure I am capable to succeed

in class I am the **minority**

I must prove myself and show them I belong here

my professor thinks my misunderstanding is rooted in my lack of effort

it is a competition between my classmates and I

I am a pea in a pod, trying to find my place

African American history is an elective

I don't know too much about my school's heritage and roots

I love my college

I am a proud graduate

I am prepared to face the real world

Randall Simone Gregory

*This is a two-voice poem, please read from left to right across both pages

College bound student 2

I am getting ready for college

everyone on campus looks like me

I am here to receive a great education

I am placed in my core classes because my ability to succeed is not in question

in class I am the **majority**

people recognize me and treat me like I'm family

my professor believes in me and ensures my hard work will pay off

my classmates and I uplift one another

I am comfortable in my skin, I've found my home

African American history is a requirement
learning my school's heritage and roots is a rite of passage

I love my college

I am a proud HBCU graduate

I am prepared to face the real world

25

Deep Hues

Black girl
black boy
you are the color of the earth
beautiful as mahogany wood
you are pretty as sienna
sweet like cinnamon rolls
you are robust as coffee beans
rich like chocolate
you are deep as the soil
savory like ginger
you are strong like an oak tree
pure as cocoa
you shine like copper
gleam like bronze
you are intricate as a Rubik's Cube
bright as hazel
gritty as the sand
you are warm like an auburn sunrise and sunset

oh, black girl
oh, black boy

you are
wholesome,
elegant,
grounded,
stable,
complete
you are the key to healing
the security blanket I hold close
you are the foundation of everything I believe in

black girl, you are me
black boy, you are him
and we will always be one

Heavy Weight

If you took away
all of the contributions
black people made
would America still be standing?

America
likes to stand on our backs

as if
we are merely the stepping stone
that leads them to success

you're welcome anyway

'Twas the Night before Class

the preparation is a ritual
got my notebook
folder
blue and black pens
that's about all I'll need
I'll put it in my bag
before I leave in the morning

I hope I get out of class early
I pray I'll make some new friends
and there better not be a first day quiz

rummaging through my closet
picking out my jewelry and accessories
laying out tomorrow's fit
gotta make sure I got the right bag to match the look

fresh kicks
on the first day are a must
hair just got done
the brothers' cuts will be so fresh
we can still see the barber's chalk outline

I heard at HBCUs
they dress like it's a fashion show
every day of the week
so that means
I gotta come with the drip

so anxious
I can barely sleep
I scroll through Instagram
until I grow tired
I got class at 9 AM
I guess I better get some sleep

A Different World

When I miss my HBCU

I watch "A Different World"

in college

I lived in a different world

far different than where I came from

in a different world

I wasn't the target

I wasn't considered a joke

nor was I disregarded

in a different world,

I'm not less than the standard of beauty

my kinky, curly, coily, hair isn't considered ugly

my education is always honored and respected

in a different world

I am a Painite crystal

brown

rare

brilliant

unfortunately,

I live the real world

far different from the one I was made from

Word to my Ancestors

Dear ancestors:
you are the reason
my wildest dreams continue to come true

your prayers protect me
through every storm
I'm learning
to be a prayer warrior just like you

you guide me
on the right path
showing me
how to be a leader
I'm following near your footsteps
while making my own

I am forever grateful
for the legacy you left behind
I will take it on as beneficiary

I'm still reading the blueprint
using all the knowledge
bestowed upon me

when I complete my mission
here on earth
I hope my impact surmounts
the mountains of amazing feats

I won't disappoint
your achievements won't be in vain
I'm ready to answer the call
an astounding destiny waits

Imitated

The curls of my hair,

the fullness of my lips,

the sway of my walk,

the shape of my hips,

the shade of my skin,

the bat of my eye

steal my blackness

but escape my experience

only wanting to be black

when it's convenient

until

you have to actually be it

Confused

How am I supposed to know

my black

is beautiful

when society teaches me

my skin is unsightly

Most days,

I remember

what grandma told me

some days,

I believe

what the media has shown me

leaving me confused

between

what has been perpetuated about me

versus

what has been instilled in me

Probate Szn

Near the end of the semester
a campus full of exhilaration
cryptic signs posted
a date
a time
a place

classified information
finally released
speculation lingers all over the school
theories stated
based on class absences

the unveil of its newest members
a tribal ritual
ready to erupt

filled stadiums
crowed buildings and areas
convocation won't be filled
but
we will be deep at a probate
the only thing we will be early
and on time for

euphoria drifting
while we wait
posters full of glitz and glamour
gleaming number balloons
floating in the crowds
so you know who they came to represent
multiple girls cheering for the same man
others reppin heavy for their set

watching the clock
looking in the distance
hoping they are near

here they come
astonishing regalia
representing historic organizations
masquerade masks
gloves
glasses
pearls
collars
and scarves

hair cuts
sweated out pressed hair
dress shoes
to kitten heels
and stomping boots

in awe
we watch and listen
ceremonial chants
serenades
songs
skits
and steps

new identities unmasked
the neos are now the talk of the town
I look forward to tomorrow's yard show
home of Black Greek Life
my favorite time of the year
probate season has arrived

Club Woody

This is Noooo ordinary place
here we make our own rules
there is no need for a DJ
the party is just getting started
after 10 the place is lit

you must have your ID
to be granted entrance into this facility
your ID will be confiscated
if they notice your card belongs to someone else
the top floor is the quietest
the main floor and lower level
compete for who can be the loudest

a place
where college students can be found
any day of the week
socializing
bright lights fill the building
securing private rooms, seats, and sections
security walking around
surveying the room
making sure
they don't have to kick anyone out

the later you arrive
the more turnt up it'll be
you might be surprised
to find so much knowledge in this historic place
choose your time and floor wisely
if you want to get work done
at The Woodruff "Club Woody" library

When the Semester is Over

The stress doesn't immediately subdue
my mental alarm clock
keeps going off
reminding me of class
or
that something is due
I keep checking my final grades
as if they haven't already been submitted
it's time to
relax
rest my mind
and release
all the pent-up stress
before
I do it all over again
another chapter closed

Homecoming

Our favorite holiday
the biggest celebration of the year
what we will spend all our money on in a heartbeat
a time when I enjoy the fruits of my labor

contagious laughter
happiness
true ecstasy

meeting new people
visiting beloved professors
seeing your old classmates
linking with people you shouldn't have

white tents
music
dancing
pre-planned fits

late nights
and
early mornings
your liver's arch enemy
"aye taste this"
cups full of secret concoctions

current students
young alum
old heads
greeks
our HBCU cousins
people that never attended your school

PWI folks trying to see what an HBCU is like
halftime performances
ultimate bliss
streams of Africa exuding from the drums
the band playing our most treasured songs
an ambiance of excellence swaying in the crowds
our ancestor's spirits resurrected through sound

food trucks
standing in l-o-n-g lines
the most exquisite art sold
fluffy funnel cakes
divine turkey legs

our annual family reunion
it is the REAL cookout
outsiders always trying to invite themselves
being reunited on your old stomping grounds
it is "y'all know what team is winning?"
circulating around
school pride present
an ebony paradise

disclaimer
from ALL the HBCU delegates
no,
you're not invited
to the celebration
if you disrespect
our sacred education

Fried Chicken Wednesday

Off to the student center

down
    the
        stairs we go

my favorite day of the week
a perfect way to get through Hump Day
it's Fried Chicken Wednesday!

five-
    more-
        minutes-

until that silver door rises
a gateway
between starving bellies and nourishment

a sea of people spew into the building
lines as long as a Jordan shoe release

rustling papers
and rummaging through bags for student IDs
the golden ticket to get in

as the gateway opens
we rush inside like Jesus' disciples
after He parted the Red Sea

upon entrance
the robust scents of
ancestry
soul
heritage
intertwined with love
like a quilt made by grandma

those rich aromas fill our noses
and follow with every footstep

the good plates are out
a room full of southern cuisine

golden fried chicken
hearty collard greens
decadent mac and cheese
wholesome white rice and beans
don't forget that angelic square of golden cornbread

with plates piled high
surveying the room for a table
a place to sit down and eat
running to get the hot sauce and ranch

while someone stands guard at your divine throne
the rush to the silverware
before the supply is gone

endless drink options
to chase down your meal

returning back to your throne
ready to smash
you have everything you need

now we feast
as African kings and queens

Dear Harriet

Were your bones made of steel?
how did you do it?
did you ever feel free?
were you always running?
how scared were you?
what should I call your superpower?
how did the stars guide you home?
did your feet ache?
did fear flutter in your stomach like butterflies?
how heavy was the load you carried?

humanity is indebted to you
freedom loves you
equality adores you
and
Dear Harriet, I thank you

Situationships

They feel like an honorable mention,

coming in second,

working for free,

the wave without the tidal,

investing in stock you know nothing about,

the participation award,

an internship with no stipend,

just experience

when the situation came

I should've jumped ship,

but I stayed aboard,

smitten to lack of commitment

now I'm drowning

Recovering Addict

Addiction...

a fact or condition of having a dependency to a particular substance, thing, or activity

my addiction consisted of mending the fragmented pieces of the man I loved

I took on the job as lead surgeon, hoping I could give him a fighting chance

no matter what it cost me

I was convinced he was worth the risk

when I billed him

he paid me in I - O - U everything

when he returned he brought an empty checkbook

his next payment was in, "I got you next time"

and the time after that it was just empty pockets

that he filled with his broken promises

his recovery went slowly

told me he was in need of another surgery

the pain continued to return

and I didn't want him to hurt

as he healed, I became broken

debt called to collect

so I took out a loan

I bet on some luck

then I gambled away my spirit just to keep his light on

a year went by and forbearance came

my spirit was in bankruptcy

my heart ended in foreclosure

when they came for repossession

I gave up the last of my afflictions

addiction...

it will take your life,
turn it outside in
and wear it as collateral damage
by the time you realize it
it's hard to fix what's happened

Homesick

There are many days
where I find myself

missing the other pieces
of myself

the pieces who made me
who I am

I can't wait to see my family
and
be reunited again

School Daze

An expansion of the mind
constant studying
inducted into adult life
somehow locating just enough time
to get assignments done
there's a turn up every day of the week
daily decisions are made
balance is critical
limited hours of sleep
wishing I appreciated naps as a kid
maybe I'd have more energy
locating professors during office hours
papers, projects, assignments, quizzes, and tests
saying I'm going to drop out every week
even though I'm on my way to class
sleepless nights
cramming sessions before a big test
happy days filled with sunshine
exhausting days full of cloudy skies
adapting to professor's teaching styles and accents
receiving tests back not knowing how you passed
other times not understanding how you didn't
wondering why your professor couldn't be a little more lenient

campus involvement
attending events
volunteering and shaping the community
learning from mistakes
advocating for self in times of need
making friends and losing friends
talking to random people on campus
signing the role and sometimes for friends
facing the hardest classes
trying to make it out alive
remembering C's get degrees

higher education will push you
it's guaranteed to change your life
yet, I wouldn't change this experience for anything

Unassigned Assigned Seat

Three days
after the semester begins
I've claimed this seat

do not sit
in my unassigned assigned seat
an unspoken rule
most understand
but
there are a few
offenders, seat hopers, and nomads

it's the one thing that annoys me
more than my professor taking a month to grade my test
problem is
when you sit
in my unassigned assigned seat

I must seize
the nearest thing next to me
siting extremely close
staring you down
giving you the side eye
the entire class

this isn't a game I want to play
your authoritarian ways
have interrupted my learning feng shui

next class
I'll be early
a battle of musical chairs commenced
and I plan to be champion
go
find another place to sit

Joseph E Lowery

When I heard the news
a sea of sadness
crashed over my eyes
and collided with my heart

a street
we all traveled
a man we were educated about

a pioneer
a flame
no longer burning
you gave us
fire
an inner heat combustion awakened

you were bright
and too strong to snuff out
now
when we ride down the street
we will say
R.I.P

a street with so much meaning
you put history
into concrete
a street traveled
by masses
marched on
by countless
we will forever
remember your legacy

especially as we ride
down
the Boulevard
we call
Joseph E Lowery

Planted

I am deeply planted
I stand firm against all odds
for those who believed
I didn't have the capabilities to grow

just know
I believe in my branches
and the direction of
the path
and when
they see I've made it
the feeling will be unfathomable

eternally, I am planted
spiritually, I am planted

gracefully walking in my purpose
I am planted

AUC

The Atlanta University Center
unlike any place on earth
highly educated cousins
all here for one purpose
striving for our degrees
all while living
in close proximity

cross registration
so we can experience each other's classes
the joy we have
when we celebrate as one

we are a trifecta
sometimes a quartet

just remember
there's no
AUC
without
CAU

*With family love to Morehouse, Spelman, and Morris Brown College.
Welcome back Morris Brown.

Persevere

When will there be change
when will freedom reign
when it's not just a saying
how long must we withstain
there's so much pain
while trying to break out of these chains
they treat me with disdain
instead of humane

Reminiscing

I still have that sticker I got on campus

the sticker that says

"Mike Brown Can't Vote, but I Can"

every time

I look at it

it reminds me

to cherish being able to breathe

because there are

tooooo

many people who can't

since society

N

    E

      V

        E

         R

gave them

a fighting chance

Picture Day

A monumental moment
a milestone his mother would remember forever
a photographer took interest in him
he was the perfect model
he had poise
lines of symmetry
and a unique look
this was the first professional picture taken of the young man
the cameraman snapped every angle of him
his body was outlined in chalk
which illuminated around him like a halo
his skin kissed the ground he once played hopscotch on
blood spilled against the cool cement
his pictures made the morning news
a father figure to his brother
a slain hero to his sister
to the police he was just another thug
who got a bullet for all the things he had done
on his birthday, his grave was already dug

*In loving memory of Mike Brown. As I prepared for college, he prepared for
Picture Day.

The Promenade

The pathway to class
a place for leisurely strolls
a fashion runway
a seller's paradise
a meet up location
a gathering place

the Illustrious stomping grounds
the before and after spot
the food truck's first stop

free sample Heaven
our favorite chill spot

where many loiter
where a celebrity can always be found

here
on campus
many memories are made

a magical carpet molded of concrete
a metamorphosis trail

you must walk this legendary ground
the places it will lead you?
you must
find out for yourself

The Infamous Question

When you ask me
where is Clark Atlanta University?
I want to be done
with the conversation
I wonder is it out of habit
or ignorance

when you ask me that question
I wonder if your context clue radar is hard of hearing
or just broken
it's as if the location isn't in the name
I think
please put some *respeck* on my
institution's name
instead
I proudly and politely say
"Clark Atlanta University is located in Atlanta, Georgia"

and then there are some
with the nerve
to say
"Oooh I've been to Morehouse and Spelman before
is Clark-Atlanta close by?"

I laugh inside
I shake my head
and think
no, you haven't!

Legend has it

There once was a man
who wore the most luxurious suits
he was always color coordinated
from his head to his toes
his upscale attire was bold yet vibrant
it was like he came from an old-school movie
he wore the most exuberant fabrics of
silk, cotton, leather, cashmere, and fur
his crown was a brim hat
that had a lone feather
no matter the weather outside
he was fully clothed
legend has it he was an old professor
some people say he attended CAU back in the day
others claimed he was wealthy
he never said too much to the people that saw him
he would just sing inaudible tunes
when he walked
each step he took was distinctive
people would stop and stare
as he glided down the concrete runway
they recorded his every move and snapped photos of him
he walked as if no one was watching
he knew his style and undeniable swagger was unmatched
there was no competition when he walked the runway
legend has it they didn't know where he came from
or where he was going

everyone just knew when he was there
the man's "true identity" is still unknown

we call him
the Promenade Pimp
when will he return?
no one knows...
but he will be back

Toxic Relationship

You keep pushing me away
I don't understand
what do I have to do
to get through?

when I call
you never pick up
I wait
hours
just to talk to you
just for you
to tell me
you simply need a break

"come back" you say
then you'll be ready to talk
and then I realized
you are capable of giving more,
but you keep giving me the cold shoulder

I've tried to be patient,
but my patience is running thin
my heart races every time I hear your line ring

one conversation could fix everything
between us
I dedicate my whole day to you
and this is how you repay me?

words can't describe the frustration I feel right now

I'm ready to give up
I can't keep fighting with you
but somehow, I can't let you go

I'm questioning
do the good days outweigh the bad?

I'll never forget the things you did for me
that's why I'm here giving you another chance

now I can't get through to you
and your phone stopped ringing
did you block my number?

you must want to see me grovel
is that what it is?
you think this is a game?
why don't you take my needs seriously?

so you really don't care?
and you think you're going to ignore me-
and I'll go away?
trust and believe
you haven't seen
or heard
the last of me
I'll have the last word

if I burn down your place, will that get your attention?
if I cuss you out, will you hear me then?

soon as we break ties
you'll be asking me-
to give back all you gave me

I know I made a promise
but honestly
how do I break it off?

all I ever wanted
was for you to support my dreams
I guess this relationship was conditional

in six months
when I've moved on with my life
I know you'll be back

then,
I won't be answering your calls
and we'll see
how you like that

I am trapped…
in a toxic relationship
with Financial Aid
I hope my *degree* is worth it!

Change

Discrimination,

seen in our nation
for generations
ignorance
further leads to our separation

I have hope
I'll reunite us all
I won't rewrite history on the wall
I have no desire to
but
I'll do my best
to write us a better squeal

Astonished

There are classes

that I can't believe

someone took their time to make

like math, physics, and organic chemistry

oh how

I despise you over achievers

that had nothing better to do

so now I'm up stressing

over this subject

all day and night

when I'd rather be sleeping

or

just busy living my life

Uno and Spades

One thing I know
we make up our own rules
they made us follow along to rules
far too long
rules we never agreed to

now
we take pride in making our own decisions
we make other people's everything better
more fun
creative
extremely competitive

every place you go
you better determine the house rules
before you play
a game of Uno and Spades

Undisclosed Tuition

My professor's salary
my tuition paid for it
so no-
I don't want to see your teaching assistant

the buildings on campus
my tuition paid for it
so yes-
I better see some renovations

the bathroom tissue
my tuition paid for it
so yes-
I'm taking some home

the library
my tuition paid for it
so yes-
the light bill is high
y'all run the lights 24/7

the student center
my tuition paid for it
so yes-
I'm upset when there's no place to sit

campus landscaping
my tuition paid for it
so no-
I don't think
the grass needs a cut every single week

the track
my tuition paid for it
so no-
I don't get why it's dilapidated and cracked

still
I'm wondering
what y'all doing with my tuition
it seems like a lot
then again it doesn't

somehow,
after all of that
my textbooks
aren't included
in the tuition
now, what's up with that?

Concerned Student

Have you ever
had "that" professor
that did everything in their power
to make your life hell
sometimes
I sit and think
about the catastrophic event
that broke my professor

on their worst days
when the classroom is on fire
and the professor
is lashing out
and it feels like I'm being whipped
I think to myself
"is everything okay at home?"
you know
you don't have to do this

Stolen Nightmares

One night I had a dream
when I woke up I was greeted by the door of no return
all I could see was the dark abyss in front of me
limb by limb we were tightly packed like a can of sardines
it was unbearably hot like an iron held to my skin
the room was rotting of feces, urine, and dead bodies

I couldn't see them
but I knew they were deceased
the way I heard the bodies fall to the floor
we were competing for oxygen molecules like it was a sport
not enough air for us all to breathe

I tried to drink the sweat off my body
but the taste of salt continued to make me thirsty
I made it out of holding
baptized in the name of their evils
dragged to the boat through torment in chains
the ocean winds whipped me

when I made it aboard
from that moment forward
I knew I would never return
to my homeland
my dignity forever buried in those sands

Graffiti

Former NFL quarterback whose career was traded for the cause.

Before I left college
an artist made an eye-catching
ever-captivating
mural of Colin Kaepernick

beautifully painted in
red
white
blue
and of course midnight black

the beautiful colors of the flag
woven with a brutal history
makes me hesitant
to pledge my allegiance

there he was silently shouting
from an abandoned building
once a desolate bando

now physically transformed with painful beauty
under the layers of sprayed make-up
the surface of raw emotions remain unchanged
yet the artist made a way to carefully highlight
complicated curves

a powerful message
encompassed with
an alteration
revised history to fit a lie
a conversion of the truth
like a new tattoo still red and swollen
throbbing with pain
bricks transposed as skin
a new identity
for just a short while...

now the building no longer stands
the rubble is like Colin's kneel
the kneel for injustice while standing
for equality
the kneel for countless black and brown deaths
the kneel for distorted humanity
and others that followed suit

even when the building
stopped standing
it's memory stands
timeless
like a skyscraper
looking down
wondering...
why justice is for some
but not for all?

Crushin'

You are a spectacle on campus
you stand out without trying
I am loyal to only crushing on you
I claim you as mine, to all my friends

when you answer a question
I melt at the sound of your voice
the sparkle in your eyes
fill me with wonder
they make me want to stargaze in the daylight

the cadence of your voice
makes my legs forget their purpose
when you walk
I imagine us strolling on a beach
by the sunset hand in hand

I've admired everything about you
I wonder what our life could be like
if you were more than a crush
I hope you are how I imagined
I'd be hurt to see you any other way

lingering thoughts
hold me back from making a move
deep down inside I wonder
if you ever felt the same
or even know my name

HBCU Hustlas

Photographers
designers
business men
hair stylists
make-up artists
social media influencers
models
nail techs
trappers
actors
actresses
lash techs
writers
promoters
business women
bottle girls
scammers
barbers
forex traders
salesmen
rappers
brand ambassadors
djs
researchers
poets
singers
entrepreneurs
painters
event planners
civil rights activists
artists
producers
dancers
phone repair technicians

meanwhile
everyone is getting an education
I love every bit of it
you name it
I guarantee someone does it

A Set up for Failure

Studying
in your bed
on a late night
you can assume
who will win
the match every time

from siting up right
to laying down
still trying to read
the same paragraph
over and over again

the final push
of your books off the bed
the whimsical crash
of them falling to the floor
the sound
that declares
your bed has won
this round

Harmony

I write my words down
in the form of poetry
when I keep reading it
it sounds like a beautiful song
I'm still learning the words
so eventually
I won't just be listening
I'll be singing along to every word
with every cadence
hearing all of the melodies my heart plays
understanding each lyric
that made me who I am

What I Wanted vs What I got

Buying your own school supplies

is a humbling experience

the tools that aid in my success

are a tad bit expensive

especially, my beloved name brands

I realize

my standards can be lowered

with the right price attached

those notebooks and pens

serve the same purpose

the only thing that stands in my way

is preference

and

the lack of money in my pocket

I Tried

I tried out for the talent show twice
I wasn't picked
from that point on
I was afraid
afraid of rejection
showing the art

suddenly questioning
if my message mattered in the first place
those thoughts still resurface
but I ignore the feeling
as much as possible
it helps me take risks

it's how I published this book
the dancing thoughts
"am I good enough"

I located my courage
laced up my kicks
sprinted to the finish line
here I am cutting the ribbon
I did more than try
Momma
I made it

Tea

Consumed

hot or cold

either way is fine

the requirement is

it must be sweet

tasting

like a cup full of diabetes

To Whom it may Concern

Dear Sallie Mae, sister of the Government
FASFA, brother of the system
and all of your other friends, cousins of oppressors
I forgave myself
from this debt
before I took out the loan
God forgives all
and you should too

Devotion

Friendship is like a delicate flower
water her,
not too much
give her nutrients,
just enough
she needs to thrive
make sure
you give her sunlight
words of encouragement
truth and honor
and seeds of love
or
she will wither away
and die

Discovery

I found life's purpose
through opportunity
hardships
learning
and discipline

then planted my seeds of experience
deep into the soil
eventually
they blossomed into my destiny
now I have everything
I need
to succeed

Letter for an Angel

Dear Alexis Crawford
my sweet fallen
black panther
I'm sorry we couldn't protect you
I'm sorry traitors desecrated
our sacred land
we're hurt by your story
we mourn as a community
I'm sorry
you never got to physically walk that grand stage
may your memory live on in our fabric
forever
and always
even through your pain
my sweet fallen
fellow black panther
you remind us
of strength
told your story
uncovering truths
we will continue to honor you
we will continue to tell your story
even if we can't hear it from you
we will never forget you
angel gone too soon

Imposter Syndrome

An irrational feeling
I suffer from
far too often
a red devil on my shoulder
trying to convince my angel
I'll never be enough
an internal battle
I want to conquer

11:59

A deadline that gives me anxiety
some college students' worst fear
our dance partner

a time
showing you can write a seven-page paper in a few hours

a time
I've missed
hoping my professor will reopen the assignment

a time
that tells me I have enough room for a nap

a time
that means I'm going to submit at 11:55

a time
that taught me I can do all things by 11:59

Spring Break Code

Untold stories
truth be damned
secrets
on top of
secrets
turn up
on top of
turn up
just take the Fifth
till death do us part
what happens on the trip
stays on the trip

Lesson Learned

As a freshman
my school taught us
an important lesson
know your requirements
for graduation
inside and out
like you know the back of your hand
like the spelling of your name
and home address

if you know this
and pass all your classes
you will graduate
on time
just remember
the future you want
is always
in your hands

Impossible

At times
my dreams feel untouchable

like the sky I can't reach
no matter how hard I try

the glass ceiling won't break
blocked from the other side
it's not meant for me
hopefully one day it will be

Photoshoot

At an HBCU
we are notorious
for our graduation photoshoots
accustomed to the tradition
we carry the torch
of immense fashion

no other grads
can compete
with our high caliber of excellence
beyond compare
we exude our supremacy

at an HBCU
the photoshoot
is just as important as the degree
it's what we look forward to checking off the list
it's the last hoorah
to memorialize
a time
our greatest achievement yet

anxiously
they wait for us
to do drop the fire flicks
dressed full of drip

modelesque posing
in our fashion mogul fits
we are the *finest*
to ever do it

Graduation

The day is here
a moment I've imagined for years
there were countless times
I wondered if it would really happen
so many days I felt I couldn't make it
but
God always revealed to me otherwise

today is THE day
when my fear of defeat breaks up with me

The day
to let go of "am I good enough"

today, The day
I stand strong and tall
knowing
I am ready
prepared to face the world

there were people I lost along the way
but I found my myself

the best day of my life
a dream come true
mixed emotions of the unknown
joining the professional world
now a part of the college educated statistic

memories I will hold on to forever
the turn of the tassel
the announcement of my name
with my degree in hand
now let the real work begin

Randall Simone Gregory

Ode to my HBCU

I will miss
the love
respect
experience

you are my village
when I walked on campus
you provided me
the tribe
I was robbed of
you are Wakanda intertwined with Heaven

you taught me
tenacity
diligence
and how to find myself

showed me
my blackness is glorious
I am beautifully made without mistake

my home away from home
I am grateful for all those that came before me
I will go out in the world
making a difference
with my head held high
sharing my priceless gifts

I chased the roots of my heritage

your imprint lead me here

I'm honored you chose me

before I even knew

I won't stop

I'll keep searching for more

until we meet again…

THANK YOU

THANK YOU

THANK YOU

to my

Illustrious

H
B
C
U

List of HBCUs

Alabama A&M University
Alabama State University
Albany State University
Alcorn State University
Allen University
American Baptist College
University of Arkansas at Pine Bluff
Arkansas Baptist College
Barber-Scotia College**
Benedict College
Bennett College
Bethune-Cookman University
Bishop State Community College
Bluefield State College
Bowie State University
Central State University
Cheyney University of Pennsylvania
Claflin University
Clark Atlanta University
Clinton College
Coahoma Community College
Concordia College*
Coppin State University
Delaware State University
Denmark Technical College
Dillard University
University of the District of Columbia
Edward Waters College
Elizabeth City State University
Fayetteville State University
Fisk University
Florida A&M University
Florida Memorial University
Fort Valley State University
Gadsden State Community College (Valley Street campus)
Grambling State University
Hampton University
Harris-Stowe State University
Hinds Community College at Utica
Howard University

Huston-Tillotson University
Interdenominational Theological Center
J. F. Drake State Technical College
Jackson State University
Jarvis Christian College
Johnson C. Smith University
Kentucky State University
Knoxville College **
Lane College
Langston University
Lawson State Community College
LeMoyne-Owen College
Lewis College of Business*
The Lincoln University
Lincoln University
Livingstone College
University of Maryland Eastern Shore
Meharry Medical College
Miles College
Mississippi Valley State University
Morehouse College
Morehouse School of Medicine
Morgan State University
Morris Brown College
Morris College
Norfolk State University
North Carolina A&T State University
North Carolina Central University
Oakwood University
Paine College
Paul Quinn College
Philander Smith College
Prairie View A&M University
Rust College
Saint Paul's College*
Savannah State University
Selma University
Shaw University
Shelton State Community College- C A Fredd Campus
Shorter College
Simmons College of Kentucky
South Carolina State University

Southern University at New Orleans
Southern University at Shreveport
Southern University and A&M College
Southwestern Christian College
Spelman College
St. Augustine's University
St. Philip's College
Stillman College
Talladega College
Tennessee State University
Texas College
Texas Southern University
Tougaloo College
H. Councill Trenholm State Community College
Tuskegee University
University of the Virgin Islands
Virginia State University
Virginia Union University
Virginia University of Lynchburg
Voorhees College
West Virginia State University
Wilberforce University
Wiley College
Winston-Salem State University
Xavier University of Louisiana

* A fallen HBCU
** An HBCU working on regaining accreditation

A Note from the Author

I wrote Chasing the Roots of my Heritage to pay homage to historically black colleges and universities. This poetry book is an ode to HBCUs. HBCUs were founded due to perpetuated stereotypes, prejudice, and discrimination. Free African-Americans were continually denied admission into predominantly white institutions because of institutionalized racism. Despite the unjust treatment, when HBCUs were founded, black people made their own sacred education. These institutions gave everyone the opportunity to be accepted, loved, and educated. I, too, know the feeling of people seeing me as "less than" just because of my skin color. I wanted to give words to an extraordinarily indescribable experience at an HBCU. It was really important for me to touch on my growth I experienced. Also, telling the common stories of what it feels like to be black in America. As a result of slavery, we were robbed of our heritage and roots. Hence the title, Chasing the Roots of my Heritage. I wanted to create something that could be passed down for generations like an heirloom. My ancestors found a way to pass on history, resilience, stories, and songs. This is my way to honor them. Now, it is my turn to pass on this book to you. Keep chasing… I know there is so much more to uproot.

ABOUT THE AUTHOR

Randall Simone Gregory

Randall was born and raised in a suburb of Cleveland, Ohio. Randall attended the Illustrious Clark Atlanta University where she earned her B.S. in Biology. She is currently a graduate student at Kent State University studying for her MPH in Epidemiology. Randall is a proud member of Alpha Kappa Alpha Sorority, Inc. Her goal is to become a pediatrician and poet that offers healing in all forms. Eventually, Randall would like to open her own children's hospital. As she will tell anyone that asks her about attending an HBCU, "It's the best decision I could've ever made." This is Randall's debut poetry book and it will certainly not be her last.

You can follow her on IG@Rsg_2poetry

Randall Simone Gregory

Made in the USA
Columbia, SC
23 April 2024